The Histories
Selected Poems from *Annum Poetica*

Titus Naso

Tomis Press

The Histories
Titus Naso

Published by Tomis Press
Silverton, Oregon

Hardcover ISBN: 978-1-958337-06-6
Paperback ISBN: 978-1-958337-22-6
E-book ISBN: 978-1-958337-23-3

The poem, "On Samuel Taylor Coleridge," was first published April 8, 2022 in the literary journal, *Teach. Write. A Writing Teacher's Literary Journal*. Katie Winkler, editor. ISBN 9781435796706

Titus Naso is a pen name of Jesse S. Smith.

titusnaso.com • tomispress.com • jessesmithbooks.com

Poetry / Biographies / History / Current events

Introduction

At the height of the pandemic lockdowns early in the year 2020, I was reading *Fasti*, a collection of poems about the Roman calendar and holidays written by the poet Ovid, who was exiled to Tomis on the Black Sea by the Emperor Augustus Caesar in the early years of the Common Era, two millennia ago.

Inspired by Ovid's work, I challenged myself to write a poem a day for the next year. As my project progressed, Ovid became my mentor, and my poem-a-day project helped me through a memorable and historic time of chaos, uncertainty, social unrest, and awakening.

Selected from that year of poetry, these are the poems about historical persons: poets and Emperors, engineers and physicists, politicians and planters. Many of the poems relate to themes of self-realization and overcoming one's limitations.

Limitations are for overcoming.

I hope these poems will inspire you.

Peace,
Titus Naso
April 2, 2022

Finding Our Way

Johnny Appleseed

A story I would like to tell today
about a man who once did something great.
No, he was not involved in politics;
some say he was just a bum in the sticks.
Important he became for planting trees:
the legendary Johnny Appleseed.

This Johnny Appleseed he wandered far,
across the land (he did not have a car)
and brought with him the seeds for which he's named,
he planted them in wilderness untamed.
He planted apple trees on hill and vale,
and round the campfire he would tell a tale
about how he had learned to love the trees
in this his home, the great land of the free.
(Just what his tale was, I now wish I knew;
if I made one up, it would not be true.)

John Chapman was his name when he was born,
he was well-loved for kindness and for more.
He wore a cooking-pot upon his head,
he gratefully accepted floor for bed
when he would tell his stories quite all right
and stay in strangers' houses for the night
as used to be the custom in those days
before people were so fearful always.

He was a man of deep godly beliefs,
and as he wandered, to the folks he'd preach
about behavior that becomes a man
and the best ways of caring for the land.

Horse-loads of seeds he planted, yes, it's true:
so many seeds they filled up two canoes!
From cider-pressers he collected seeds,
and in this way, he got them all for free.

Some say Johnny Appleseed liked to drink
hard apple cider, and this made him think,
"Apple trees should be spread across the land
  so cider hard will always be at hand!"
Some say that's not perfect altruism,
but I think it's nearly communism,
and for that there's still much credit due him.
For once the trees were planted, fruit would grow
for any passer-by to eat, you know:
and giving food to strangers who pass by
the model is of generosity.

It seems likely from how he is described,
he was disturbèd in his frame of mind;
and yet he was so gentle, truly kind,
that friendly faces he could always find.

So from Johnny let us example take
of how a better world we all might make:
with kindness to each other we may please,
and show love to the Earth by planting trees!

Albert Einstein

Albert Einstein once second-guessed himself,
announced his equation was incorrect:
the 'cosmological constant' he'd used,
represented by Greek letter 'lambda' (Λ)
had been an error, as he now believed
based on Edwin Hubble's discoveries
of an ever-expanding universe.
But decades later, long after he'd died,
astrophysicists revived old 'lambda'
to account for the acceleration
of that same universal expansion.
Einstein, it turned out, was right the first time:
his error lay in thinking he was wrong.
Have faith in yourself! Don't ever give up:
for you, too, may someday be proven right
by poorly understood Dark Energy.

Emily Dickinson

Emily Dickinson was a recluse:
the poet did not like to leave the house,
and no one knew how she put time to use.
Her poetry she rarely talked about.
Although she sometimes sent poems to her friends
she never boasted, or tried to publish,
and she collected them for unknown ends –
was posthumous publication her wish?
She did the work and compiled the material
and there it languished in a dusty chest.
Perhaps she thought it was too personal,
and abandoning it was for the best?
Her work, now priceless, came at such a cost;
we all are fortunate it was not lost!

Susan B. Anthony

Beginning with her work 'gainst slavery
she was always to justice devoted,
and for her passion for equality
these many years later she is still noted.
She also joined campaigns 'gainst alcohol
with Elizabeth Cady Stanton her friend.
Forced to create their own group after all,
when for gender, speaking engagement was banned.
Through decades of speaking, she awareness raised
for the plight of women, who had no vote –
promote equality, her name be praised,
let all the children learn her tale by rote!
For few've helped change so much in history
as our hero, Susan B. Anthony.

Amanda Gorman

Amanda Gorman! 'Tis thy name we praise
shining thy light in these brightening days,
reminding us in the Land of the Free
transformational pow'r of poetry.
Your speech at Biden's inauguration
deeds your place in the hist'ry of our nation.

Casey Jones

Casey Jones once rescued a little girl
who had stopped on the train tracks, petrified,
too terrified to get out of the way
as the locomotive barreled towards her.
Jones happened to be oiling relief valves
when he saw the child who'd stopped on the tracks.
He shouted to his fellow engineer,
"Throw it into reverse, Bob, quickly now!"
and raced forward along the running board
to the cattle catcher at the train's front.
He clambered out to the tip of the train
as it approached the petrified small child.
Perched, clinging tight to the front of the train,
he leaned forward over the railroad tracks
and stretched forth his arms to pluck the young child
out of harm's way at the final moment,
swinging her onto the train that she feared –
a mere fraction of a second before
the story would have ended tragically
had Casey Jones not been so brave that day
and fearlessly risked his own life to save
a complete stranger from Fate's certain death.
But that act of heroism is not
what Casey Jones is best remembered for.

It's for the way he died his name lives on,
the most famous of the steam engineers.
It matters not if he was sleep deprived,
his work was top notch anyway.
(He certainly was not high on cocaine,
 as the Grateful Dead in their version claim;
 they just said that because it rhymes with "train"
 and not because there's truth to that refrain!)
But true it is, 'twas late into the night
as Casey Jones was at the train's controls.
He did not see flag-waving signal man
obscured by fog and night – the train sped on,
the train they called the Cannonball, so fast
did it hurtle along the railway line,
and Casey Jones meant to make up lost time
to compensate for late departure;
for by getting his runs to the station
on time, he would someday advancement earn,
or so he hoped – and so he sped, too fast –
yes, Casey Jones was known to be reckless.

Seventy-five miles per hour 'round the curve
the Cannonball careened, when through the rain
emerged the shape of train cars suddenly:
a freight train, stalled, stuck, and stationary
there on his line, in front of his own train;
and the passing track had been occupied
by double-header freight train 83
and infamous freight train 72.
They blocked his path. He knew what he must do.

Though he instructed his colleague to jump,
he did not even think to run away,
but pulled with all his might on the air brakes,
and threw the engine's throttle in reverse
so braking pow'r from the engine he'd gain.

Wheels locked, the train skidded along wet tracks,
Casey wrestled with the controls and tugged
with all his might upon the brake lever
even as he saw the stalled cars approach.
Casey's steam engine plowed through four freight cars,
but ultimately he was successful
in slowing the train. There was but one death.
All the passengers aboard that train lived.
The only person who died on that night
was the bravest of railway engineers:
Casey Jones, who saved a train full of folks
at the cost of his own life. What a guy.

Robert Frost

You were an icon, genius of your time.
Your era spanned great upheaval and change.
You wrote blank verse, but you're best known for rhyme;
your creativity had quite a range.
You wrote of horse-drawn cart in snowy woods,
you wrote of firewood chopped and stacked by hand.
Your allegories asked what makes us good,
your stories showed a deep love for the land.
You took the road less traveled – poetry –
and spoke of the destructive ice of hate.
Your wisdom and your pain inspire me,
broad int'rests and learning make your work great.
From ev'ry word of your poetic lines
your love for land and Nature truly shines!

Abraham Lincoln

'Twas seven score and sixteen years ago
when he became a martyr to his cause.
The leader who brought slav'ry to an end
then gave his life for what he had achieved.

A rags-to-riches story; but it's true!
A boy who in a log cabin was raised
and taught himself from textbooks found in trash
succeeded in becoming someone great.
A lawyer, well-respected in his town,
he was elected to State government,
for four terms to the Illinois State House
before he was elected to a seat
of Fed'ral government, the U.S. House.
The prominence helped him spread his ideas
and drew attention to good Abraham.
A candidate of compromise he was:
'twas on the third ballot his name rose up.
Electors then chose Lincoln President!

But in the South, they had other ideas:
no compromise was possible with them.
From Union they most haughtily withdrew,
and fired the war's first shots on Fort Sumter.
Tho peaceful Lincoln had not this desired,
he understood his duties all too well
to country, liberty; to God and man;
and thus he chose the Union to defend
against the mad aggression of the South.

Th' Emancipation Proclamation did
grant freedom to the slaves across the South:
a late triumph for justice, with no teeth
given the state of war there at that time.
Thus liberty's progress imperfect is,
by fits and starts, backsliding and great grief,
yet nonetheless, we hold to our ideals!

An army raised and fought for four hard years
with devastating weapons. Much had changed,
and warfare's tactics lagged behind the times.
A hundred thousand died at Gettysburg
in just a single day of fighting there.
On back of envelope, riding the train,
Lincoln composed his most famous Address.

Equality became the law at last
in 1865, when ratified
Amendment the Thirteenth at last became.

The bloody Civil War ground to an end.
At Appomattox Gen'ral Lee gave in,
admitting that he had suffered defeat.

But Lincoln did not long survive the peace.
He went to see a play, and was gunned down.
We celebrate good Abraham today,
the man who brought an end to slavery
(although it had not been his object first).
His core belief that Union must prevail
has shaped these great United States today!

George Washington

When his ideals and country called to him,
he did not shirk: he stepped up and went forth,
and in that role he changed our histōry.

A wealthy man with plantation and slaves,
he served under the Brits in his first war
against the French and allied Native tribes
who hoped to drive the settlers from these shores
(tho it had been too late since e'er they came).
The British won that war, but at what cost?
To pay for it, they taxed the Colonies –
for after all, it was the Colonies
who, one might argue, benefited most.
Americans rebelled against that tax.

George Washington was asked to lead the troops
based on the reputation he had built
in politics, as well as his service.
He led those troops for 8 long years of war,
and used guerrilla tactics 'gainst the sieges
the British laid on Boston and New York.
It was a long shot 'til the French joined in;
but in the end, the British sailed on home,
"To hell with Yankee Doodle and his cap!"

But time passed, and all was precarious.
The government its vet'rans could not pay,
and Washington squatters could not evict.
So Washington backed government reforms,
and stood he for the role of President
the which he did attain for eight key years.

He set the tone for governing by law,
and at the end of his term, he stepped down
and thus a great example he did set
for power's transfer in a peaceful way.
For this, we praise his memory today!

Robespierre

Tho Robespierre was only a symptom,
    I am glad he is dead;
For no one has ever deserved so much
    to lose his bloody head.

Johannes Kepler

A sickly, intellectual young boy
Johannes Kepler was, the night he saw
the Great Comet blazing through the night sky.
Surely it sparked love for astronomy,
as did a lunar eclipse he observed –
for one who has seen comet and eclipse
understands there is much we do not know.
Kepler studied at a monastery,
but did not join the order, and instead
he became a mathematics teacher.

Soft-spoken and easily distracted,
perhaps not an ideal schoolmaster he.

But Kepler was a man who had ideas,
intricate solar system models built
based on the theories of Copernicus
whose famous paper was fairly recent
and still a source of great controversy –
so much so, the pow'r hungry Catholic Church
of Kepler demanded, he must convert!
"The Universe *does* revolve around us,"
the Church insisted. "We are important!"
But the Church was wrong about many things.
Kepler refused to say what they wanted,
and he was punished for his free thinking.
It's not easy to believe in the truth,
in a world full of people who love lies.
Exiled from his home, he was forced to leave,
and brought along his wife, who despised him.

They made their way to Tycho Brahe's court,
an endless party filled with gross intrigue
led by flamboyant golden-nosed Brahe.
Unhappy was Kepler in his exile,
and did not play well with the other dolphins;
but Brahe was an astronomer, too,
and he'd made accurate observations,
noting the "erratic" orbit of Mars.

On his deathbed, Brahe's repeated wish:
"Oh, let me not seem to have lived in vain!"
His astronomical observations
gave meaning to Tycho Brahe's wild life:
Kepler plugged them into calculations
and with math proved Copernicus correct....
except for that erratic Mars orbit!

which forced Kepler at length to think again.
Eventually the math made him conclude:
the planets' orbits are elliptical,
elliptical paths o'er ethereal plane,
and we distant are unaware travelers.

But Kepler's problems did not end with math.
The Luth'ran Church, just as intolerant
as the Cath'lics from whom they'd made their split,
formally excommunicated him
because he kept saying all these true things,
and people cannot tolerate the truth.

Now exiled and excommunicated,
Kepler spent much time fighting in the courts
to save his mother from execution:
for she was a healer, quite skilled with herbs,
and perhaps quarrelsome with her neighbors
(but who can blame her, really? Look around!)
Obviously, she was accused of witchcraft.
The case dragged on for six most dreadful years;
she fourteen months spent languishing in prison
while her loyal son fought bullshit charges.
People are closed-minded, petty, hateful,
and the ones who claim they're not are the worst.

The principal theory Kepler pursued
throughout his life was simply wrong. Oh, well!
His brilliant mind deduced planet orbits;
grand telescope lenses he helped refine;
and at the end, before Johannes died,
he graced the world with his science fiction,
a dream of traveling up to the Moon,
postulating people of other worlds
who were not so diff'rent from you and me.

Rev. Dr. Martin Luther King, Jr.

O for to "Love thy neighbor as thyself,"
"Love thine enemy," "Turn the other cheek,"
O for the search for peace within oneself
despite critics who love to call us "weak."
O for the spread of love unto the poor
O for a love that can transcend all race
O let us each realize we can do more
and do our work with smiles upon our face.
This was the message preached by Dr. King,
a message we recall upon this day –
a man who dared to dream the future 'ld bring
that universal love for which we pray.
So on this day let us recall his dream,
that equal rights may in the future gleam.

Oscar Wilde

Perhaps it should have surprised none
    that Oscar Wilde was bi,
for in his writings, he'd always been
    an edgy, transgressive guy.
One gets the sense there might have been
    nothing he wouldn't try.

But in those days, it was a sin,
    and worse, against the law
for a man to sleep with other men;
    it was his fatal flaw.
To prison sent for an event,
    he there saw what he saw.

But Oscar Wilde was a married man
    at the time of his disgrace;
though after that, his wife never let
    him come around the place.
No, after that, his own children
    never again saw his face.

No, moved he then far overseas
    after he was from prison released,
but he had no money of his own
    and his wife was super pissed.
No, she would not the funds disburse
    to let him live in ease.

Thus Oscar Wilde was moved to write
    a poem 'bout prison life,
and published it under a pen name
    to hide it from his wife –
he published it under his prisoner number
    from his time of toil and strife.

'Twas called, "The Ballad of Reading Gaol,"
    it was a story grim
of what he saw behind those walls
    in prison's interim
and the implied threat, as he saw
    a man hanged in front of him.

He empathized with the condemned
    who looked up at the sky
before the hangman measured him
    and looked him in the eye
in the last moments of his life
    before he had to die.

And die he must, for it was sure
    no man could e'er do worse –
his guilt was clear, none shed a tear,
    his crime they did rehearse;
but Oscar Wilde felt sympathy,
    and wrote it in his verse.

"For each man kills the thing he loves,"
    he wrote with Irish lilt,
acknowledging we all have failed
    in this society we have built:
and therefore, if we've all done wrong,
    we all share the condemned man's guilt.

For who are we to condemn someone
    who has done something bad?
How can we say there is no way
    we'd have done the same as he had?
The fact we haven't yet found out
    should always make us glad.

No, we'll never know if we'd have done the same,
    and make us glad that must:
we can condemn the man who failed
    and gave in to his lust,
and never have to ask ourselves
    if justice is truly just.

Samuel Taylor Coleridge

Samuel Taylor Coleridge wrote a poem
the which he titled, *Dejection: An Ode*.
When I read it for a class in college
it drove me nuts. I could not understand
why anyone would want to celebrate
the negative emotions in their life.
Why not just focus on being happy?
So far went I along that train of thought,
an answ'ring poèm I was moved to write
one night in Sophomore year at 3am,
three stanzas of rhyming verse mockery,
a poem which I titled, *Kind Weed: An Ode*.
It extolled the virtues of getting high:
the buds, the baggies, and the glass bong hits.
That was my response to S.T. Coleridge.

I find myself, twenty-five-plus years on,
writing my own dejected poetry,
and sympathizing with Mr. Coleridge,
his unhappy thoughts and drug addiction.
And looking back upon his work just now,
I find I envy him his turn of phrase:
my own verse is bumbling, pedestrian;
he sings of the moon, Aeolian lute,
the ev'ning sky, the clouds and sparkling stars,
and the young woman who kept him up nights,
to whom his secret confessions he spilled
of hopeless love outside his sad marriage,
to whom his thoughts turned at the dark midnight.

I find that I had just one passage marked:
"And in our life alone does Nature live."
It struck me as quite Buddhist at the time;
it was, O Coleridge, an insightful line.

Shakespeare's Love Triangle

William Shakespeare, in his sonnets so famed
seems to be part of a love triangle,
and although the other two are not named
it's clear their lives are all in a tangle!
Although as readers consider we must,
they characters composite may have been;
there's lurking in those verses tales of lust,
deceitfulness, and treachery, and sin.
We sometimes now think it's our duty
the behavior of others to call out.
He tells the tale in words of great beauty;
but Will and friends morality did flout!
To the present time from Elizabethan Age,
human beings are totally on the same page.

A Monk of the Middle Ages

Great praises are due to Bēdē of old,
thinker and scholar, not merely a monk:
he calculated the course of the Moon
through the chart of the year, our calendar.
A great historian of his era
(few wrote hist'ries in year 700)
he recorded and compared the month names
as used in classical antiquity
to those used in his own time, as in ours;
but he also helpfully makes a note
of the ancient names given to the months
by the Hebrews, Egyptians, Macedon,
and in Celtic ancestors' Old English.

Monk Bēdē deeply cared 'bout calendars –
it was a spiritual pursuit for him,
to pore over those dusty manuscripts
most of them written in Vulgate Latin,
and eke out the secrets of the ancients,
then performing careful calculations
to figure out how the months all lined up –
he worked it out, nobody had before,
the relative correspondence of months:
calendars Roman, Egyptian, Hebrew,
Macedonian, and the Old English, too;
along with cycles of the moon and sun
so he could calculate the Holy Days
and make Easter fall in the right season:
continuity was important to him.

Bēdē was disturbed by accusations
of heresy, from Bishops above him
who did not understand, saw a challenge,
and went on the attack, as people do.
One translator even speculated
that Bēdē's work, *The Reckoning of Time*,
was a lengthy defense, justifying
earlier writings that caused him trouble.
Faith Wallace blows this idea to pieces –
The Reckoning of Time was a textbook
used to explain astronomy to monks,
with history and religion on the side.
Though Bēdē surely felt himself aggrieved,
his writing served a much greater purpose.

The Poet and the Emperor

Exiled to Tomis

Sent far away to barbarian lands,
to distant Tomis, shores of the Black Sea
among the Goths, the exiled poet stands,
his heart filled with a yearning to be free,
his mind filled with the injustice of it all.
Sent away from his home into exile,
he does what poets do: begins to write.
Protestations keep him busy the while:
he scribbles elegies into the night.
He got in trouble for something he said:
Augustus was outraged by poems of love!
Perhaps he's fortunate not to be dead
he thinks, looking upon the stars above.
He was accused of something else: we don't know quite
what his sin might have been, whether severe or trite.

Based on my personal experience
of being scapegoated by an "in group,"
I wonder if it was a circumstance
trivial, which threw Ovid for a loop:
a squabble, just some drama quite petty,
resulted in his becoming outcast.
The "reason" is not the real reason, when he
was made a symbol. He would be the last:
none else would challenge the morals rigid
after Augustus had laid down the law.
The onlookers decided to be frigid
when scapegoated Ovid's fate they all saw.
No one stood up for him, he had no defenders,
and his poems arrived in Rome, *non grata* sender.

Tristia

Ovid opens his sad oratory
in *Tristia* by addressing the book,
the book itself in which he writes his poems
and which he hopes will deliver his words
to those who have cast him out of his home,
and plead his case to soften their cold hearts.
Ovid speaks to the book as a person,
describes it, and discusses strategy:
there's no point arguing about the details,
the public has already decided,
and reviewing the facts of Ovid's case
will only remind them of their hatred.
His only hope is to find sympathy
among kind souls who might plead lenience.

You can tell that Ovid was the target
of malicious gossip, because he fears
that even if a sympathetic soul
were to pray for him, they would stay silent,
and only pray with their thoughts: otherwise,
in voicing a defense of the scapegoat
they'd find themselves the rage mob's next target.
Little has changed in these two thousand years.
Little has changed. People take joy in hate
and vindictively hurt who they notice,
showing no care for notions of justice.

I feel a kinship with outcast Ovid,
shunned, exiled, scapegoated, and derided;
and I too began my handwritten book
with a comment about the book itself,
although as always, my sentiments plod
rather than soaring with the eloquence
of the author of *Metamorphoses*.

Distress of the Heart and Mind

A bird who's been chased learns to avoid cats,
the deer in the woods run from barking dogs,
barnyard fowls flee when the hawk approaches,
and one who has been targeted by mobs
of gossip-mongers spewing hateful rage
likewise learns to avoid such companions.
Should the creative works of one distressed
be judged by the same standards as one who
is living in leisure and luxury?
Ovid, fearful of the barbarians
among whom he had been sent in exile,
the claim advances, "Why, the poet great,
  Homer himself," (who beside Shakespeare stands
as pillars of our artistic culture) –
"even Homer's talent would have failed him
  had he been made to suffer circumstance
  and times so dire: with stress, anxiety..."
and yet, we find a way to rise above:
for Ovid, while doubting the quality
of his own work, was able nonetheless
to give voice to his sentiments in poems
which, though obscure, have survived all these years...

Although a distress of the heart and mind
may hurt as badly as physical pain,
it leaves no visible bodily scars:
only wounds which we hope will quickly heal,
having embraced doctrines of forgiveness
and pursued techniques of the empty mind
(though the latter is easier said than done).

Shockingly Immoral Poetry

It would be impossible to quarrel!
The major themes of Ovid's poems of love:
one certainly could call them "immoral,"
their subject matter is shocking enough!
I know you're interested, don't put on airs:
the whole premise is illicit affairs.
The poet expounds on the theme, and shows
how to carry on under husband's nose.
It's all set forth in his *Amores*:
his diligent pursuit of love's forays
(assuming it's only *slightly* fictionalized
 rather than, as some suggest, a complete pack of lies).

Sexy Indiscretions

In his own time, Ovid became well-known
for writing several books of poems on love;
and in those poems, attention special paid
to what we now might call, "just getting laid."
His emphasis on sex made popular
his work; and people are no different now.
He talked at great length about seduction
and described the rampant affairs in Rome
where everyone was fucking everyone –
this was, after all, just after Catullus!
Thus, when Augustus learned that Julia
his daughter, many lovers had enjoyed,
including, on at least one occasion,
two men (other than her husband) at once,
somehow the Emperor affixed the blame
for his daughter's sexy indiscretions
on Ovid, because he wrote those damn poems.
Thus the writings that had made him famous
now became the cause of his ostracism –
along with an unspecified error,
as I've mentioned before, and will again.
The translating scholar named Peter Green
believes the "error" was the real reason
for Ovid's ostracism to Tomis;
and that it was most likely not an act
but a failure to act, or to report
information the poet might have known –
such as infidelities in the house
of the Emperor himself, perhaps?
Not wishing to feed the damned rumor mill,
Ovid does not specify,
leaving us to speculate.

Tales that Do Offend

One wonders how faithful Ovid has been
to sources old, when he the myths retells
in colors that have come down through the years;
for on reflection, it appears perhaps
he took delight in tales that do offend,
and t'wards that end he added viōlence
in places it had previously not been –
his version of Medusa's tale, for one.
As such, I feel I'm not obliged to give
a full recounting of details that leave
the modern reader feeling sick or sad.
We often cannot say for certain if
a story's been mangled by Ovid's poem.
So peace upon you, fam'ly; peace to ghosts;
O peace upon the people of the town;
and peace upon thee, Ovid, who sought not
offense to cause... except for when you did!

Ovid's Great Error

With speculation I have filled your ears
dear reader, as I pondered the myst'ry
of banished Ovid's exile: his secret
error, oft ref'renced, never expounded;
and his unfinished *Fasti* poems of time,
that celebration of celebrations
which only takes us through the year's first half.
Now, reading *Tristia* (translator Green),
at last I seem the answers to have found.

Apparently, that arrogant arsehole
Augustus was as bad at ruling Rome
as he was at dispensing true justice.
Not even Romans could stand Augustus.
So discontented the populace was,
a conspiracy was hatched. Julia,
daughter of the exiled royal daughter,
was herself exiled for her involvement,
her husband executed for treason.
In *Tristia*, Ovid repeats the claim
that he never took up arms, nor did he
actively foment an insurrection.
Said just once, it's literary flourish;
mentioned repeatedly, one gets the sense
that Ovid's secret crime was on those lines
but not as bad. Most likely, Green suggests,
Ovid had knowledge of conspiracy
and chose not to report, though he could have.
This is not to imply that he planned it;
only that, in failing to report it,
he became, as 'twere, an accessory.

Sent into exile, the man felt as though
'twas to his execution that he sailed.
On the eve of his journey, Ovid burned
his revised draft of *Metamorphoses*
and his rough initial draft of *Fasti*:
the second half, from July to December.
The world will never know what wit was lost
when that collection was consigned to the flames!
See *Tristia*, Book I, the 7th poem,
and weep for lost potential everywhere.

He is Home

I'd love to write a script for a movie
about Ovid at Tomis in exile.
Although the *Tristia* poems name no locals,
they tell a distinct story of despair:
the poet, sick and gaunt, depressed, crazy,
complains about his life, pisses folks off –
they do not like to hear their town slandered!
But near the end he must stand in defense,
joining the lines to repel barbarians;
and at the last, he is joined by his wife,
long-suffering and loyal to her man,
she joins him in his exile, far from Rome,
and only then does he feel he is home.

Heaven Sent

I'd like to tell the story of a man
whose name, when born, it was Octavian:
how his inherited and stolen wealth
went far to compensate for his own poor health
and, let's be frank, his cowardice.
Oh, the great fame of Caesar Augustus
no more rested on strength than on justice.
Of civil war the people grew tired;
this made them ready to welcome Empire.
He bullied his way into the great role,
murdering, thieving, lying. Not a soul
was allowed to voice dissent –
and Augustus claimed to be heaven sent!

August's Namesake

i.

This month is named after an Emperor:
Augustus, by the Senate deified.
So caught up were they in righteous fervor,
if you called him a man, they'd say you lied!
The worship of leaders is dangerous:
this is not the goal of democracy.
Let us learn a lesson from Rome's demise:
people with too much pow'r are treacherous,
they cease to pursue true equality
and ask you to disbelieve your own eyes.

ii.

Augustus is not famed for his greatness.
Although much is attributed to him,
modern thinkers must ask if this is true.
In fact, I would argue, his connection
to Uncle Julius of great renown
is the only reason we remember
Augustus, otherwise a minor man.

The Romans praised Augustus for success
in fighting foreign wars across Europe;
yet Augustus was known to be sickly,
he suffered from a weak disposition.
One pictures him, in royal pavilion,
in his soft bed with silken sheets he groans,
his belly he clutches, and he sniffles,
while outside his tent, the common soldiers
form their ranks and prepare for the fierce charge –
their captains don't ask if *they* feel okay!

I've done absolutely zero research
to back up this reputation-trashing;
but the man who exiled poor Ovid
deserves little sympathy in my eyes.
Augustus only had a claim to fame
because his uncle won the civil war
and was assassinated publicly
by Senators, in Senate's very halls,
for claiming the right to life appointment.

The famous Julius was Great-Uncle
to young, wealthy Gaius Octavius;
and the dictator named his grand-nephew
as his heir and successor, in his will.
By reading that will to the gathered crowd,
Mark Antony turned public sympathy
in favor of monarchy, foolishly,
his brain addled by Cleopatra's love.
Thus, when Antony lost a civil war in his own turn,
'twas not for democracy people's hearts did yearn.

By might people believed right was proved.
Antony, Lepidus, Octavian
met outside Rome, near Bologna encamped,
decided by force how the world would be moved;
indeed, it never was the same again.
To fully seize pow'r, they also seized wealth
appropriated from their enemies:
they named **thousands**, and deprived them of health,
as well as of life, and of liberties!
These proscriptions, the height of callousness,
as our old friend Plutarch to us describes,
consolidated pow'r, stifled dissent.
Each one sacrificed allies in this mess:
an uncle and a brother lost their lives,
and that is where honor and goodness went.

It did not end there, things got out of hand:
to appease ranks of retiring soldiers
Octavian confiscated much land –
always those less powerful he injures.
From citizens he seized
so the Army would be appeased;
but 'twas his high-profile divorce
that led to a show of force.

iii.

Because his great-uncle was Julius,
Octavian could fall back on his name,
his family connections. True it was,
fortune favored him with family fame.
Having *primo* status inherited,
Octavian did his wealth consolidate
regardless of what he may have merited:
Parthian war funds he did confiscate!
– an act illegal, but punished never,
by the Senate essentially approved;
and theft of Near Eastern tribute, clever,
as calculating Octavian moved.
Everyone loves a very wealthy man.
Now that he had stolen enough money,
the Roman soldiers loved Octavian
and he gathered his own loyal army.
By boasting of Great Julius' divinity,
Augustus won himself Roman affinity.

iv.

Positioning in politics, the core:
aligning, posturing, and taking sides,
connections unrelated drawing thus.

After the death of Caesar Julius,
Mark Antony inflamed popular outrage
against conspiring Senators murd'rous,
and thus, against democracy itself.

But even Antony had principles
relying on his own thoughts and logic.
He had known Julius as a real man,
and as such, he refused support to lend
to the too-literal hyperbole
proposal, to name Caesar as a god.
A god! Ridiculous! He was a man,
as Antony knew well, yes, all too well –
why, both of them had Cleopatra loved,
only, Antony had loved her better. ;)
But in denying his old friend's godhead,
Antony found himself losing support,
suddenly on the outs with the people
who otherwise agreed with his ideas.

His young rival, still known as Octavian,
enticed armed defectors with better pay:
so much for the loyalty of legions!
Recognizing ripening rivalry,
Antony refused to release the funds
Octavian from Caesar inherited.
Thus conflict solidified enmity.

At Phillipi, conspirators' defeat
had mostly been achieved by Antony
whose forces fierce the famous battle won.
Augustus (at the time, Octavian)
his own authority delegated
to Marcus Agrippa, the fact of which
Antony would later use to accuse
Augustus of cowardice. That's not all –

Antony further accused Augustus
of *servicing* old Julius Caesar,
sexually, to win his inheritance.
Surely this latter accusation was
nothing more than a political smear,
hyperbole, as 'twere, little light lies;
what's a little slander between old friends?

"Republic," divided amongst victors,
descended into squabbling chaos grim
as each fought others for supremacy,
'til Lepidus was exiled and brought low.

His consulship expiring, Antony
marched on Gaul, and besieged (diff'rent) Brutus
at Mutina, ignoring the Senate.
But Cicero understood alliance,
and in his speeches attacked Antony,
meanwhile slyly supporting Octavian
and urging the Senate to empower him:
and this positioning was everything.
Supported by the Senate, Octavian
marched his army to Gaul, relieving Brutus.
Defeated, Antony now retreated.
The Senate honored Brutus: he'd survived
the siege for months, awarding him status.
Octavian was pissed off about this.
He demanded both of the consulships –
two offices, meant to check and balance!
When he was refused, his army he led
straight into Rome, just as Julius had:
more or less took a consulship by force,
and through the years made that power absolute.

Mutina

O Mutina, ye mutineers,
what came to pass confirmed your fears.
O Mutina, ye mutineers,
your hopes were dashed and came to tears.
Octavian's troops to your town laid
a siege, you were in blood repaid
for daring to claim you were free:
the Romans squelched you righteously,
Octavian claimed the victory
and ended Rome's democracy.
Thus ended Rome's long civil war,
'twas freedom you'd been fighting for –
your city walls had held within
the last of those brave assassins
who'd murdered on the Senate floor
Julius who always wanted more.
But might does not mean we are right,
and crimes occur out in plain sight –
like when those Caesars broke the laws
and were rewarded with applause.
Mutina, may you take your rest:
for tho you lost, you were the best.

Imperator

Octavian was only twenty years old
when he was named Imperator of Rome
after defeating Mutina at last.
The Roman people found they much preferred
to hand their freedoms to a dictator
rather than suffer long protracted wars.
Let this a lesson be for those who say
they would pursue ideals at any cost.
There are some costs that none will gladly pay!
When war goes on too long, support is lost.

The Battle of Actium

And yet, the wars did not end at that time.
No, twelve more years would pass before the day
when Antony suffered naval defeat.
At Actium's battle of fame, he lost
his nerve, and followed Cleopatra's barge
when she unexpectedly left the ranks,
thus demoralizing all who remained,
causing the crisp crisis of confidence
which resulted in such crushing defeat.

After this episode, Antony fled
over land and sea, to Egypt exile,
until at last, cornered, he killed himself:
for Cleopatra's love could not sustain
him through the knowledge of his failures great.
Learning of his death, she killed herself, too.
Thus it was that Augustus held his power.

A Time of Turbulence

Augustus Caesar presided over
a time of turbulence in ancient world,
the incidents which set history's stage
and launched the reality we all know:
the formal end of Roman Republic
and transformation to royal Empire;
and the crucifixion of Jesus Christ,
with great consequence for world religion.

Ruthlessly He Rose

Ruthlessly he rose to power in Rome
repealing the Republic to replace
the government with an Imperial one,
himself at the head. And along the way
young Octavian was responsible
for the murder or exile of thousands,
so he could seize their wealth and quell dissent.
Rewarded for ruthlessness with riches,
he attained his goal. For goodness, go grieve!
Octavian was installed as Emp'ror
by the spineless sad sack scared Senators
who voted to honor him with titles
(such as his moniker, Augustus "wise")
and godhood – rather than run the real risk
of losing their own heads to his cruel ambition.
After him our sunny summer month's named.

The Canceling of Agrippa Postumus

Ostracizing people who've caused offense
is hardly a modern innovation;
nor was Ovid the first to incur the wrath
of that famed puritanical asshole,
angry Emperor Augustus Caesar.
Agrippa Postumus had preceded
our poet to banishment and exile.
Translator Peter Green describes this man
as an "unperson." Echoes of Orwell
are clearly intentional – relevant
today, when people are eager to hide
history of which they've become embarrassed,
and to excise any who disagree
rather than work towards an understanding.

Adopted was Agrippa Postumus
by his grandfather, Emperor of Rome.
He thus became a grand royal scion,
although without pretensions to the throne.

His mother was the famed exile, Julia
(the daughter of Augustus Caesar, she).
His sister followed him into exile
the next year: junior Julia, sent away,
her husband executed without trial.

One begins to wonder if the stories
told of 'brutish' Agrippa Postumus
are even partly true, or just cover
for darker secrets in the family feud.
Why was Agrippa sent so far away
to the tiny island of Planasia
where he was kept under heavy armed guard
by soldiers who, in due time, murdered him?

Was it because he was so quarrelsome
that Agrippa Postumus was canceled?
Was he the subject of disgrace because
he would rather go fishing than to school?
Or was he run out of town by rivals
to protect the claims of Tiberius?
Many Romans were prone to fierce fighting,
but only a few were banished for life.
It seems unlikely the rumors were true.

The family members of Augustus were
all faced with precarious uncertainty –
'twas dangerous to be his relative,
you were likely to find yourself exiled!

The madness of Augustus may have been
with calculating coldness incited
by Livia his wife, behind the scenes
talking lots of shit to manipulate
her powerful husband, all with the aim
of ensuring succession for her son
Tiberius – she'd do anything for him,
like get his rival, Postumus, exiled.

They called him brutish and temperamental,
they said that he preferred fishing to school.
Was it his human fallibility
that got Agrippa Postumus exiled
and eventually murdered by his guards?
Or was that just a convenient excuse
to remove him from Rome, well out of the way,
so he could not claim his inheritance
or challenge Tiberius' claim to the throne?
Hist'ry does not say, there's no way to know;
but I certainly have my suspicions.

July's Namesake

i.

Hail Caesar, you who were stabbed in the back
by Senators who believed in freedom –
they martyred themselves to democracy
when public sentiment favored tyrants.
Even today, the seventh month is named
after you, Julius, voted a god
by those ass-kissing cowards, posturing,
always aligning for appearances.
Perhaps it would be better if this month
were still named Quintilis for old number
rather than remember a dictator
whose civil war began the slow decline
of Rome, from the mightiest Republic
to an overstretched Empire, mismanaged,
susceptible to attack there at home
while depraved lunatics claimed leadership.
July in summer, a beautiful month,
named after a cruel egomaniac
who never should have crossed the Rubicon
had he a single shred of decency,
loyalty, or respect for Roman law.
No, Julius cared only for himself,
and so we honor him up to this day
with a salad, a blended orange drink,
and an entire month, all named after him.

ii.

My wife compels me to correct myself:
the salad is not named for Julius.
The Caesar Salad is named for the chef
who invented it: his name was Cesar.
Perhaps I should write a poem just for him,
and another for the orange juice stand guy.

The King of Numidia

Juba, Juba, Juba!
Beware the Sixth of April –
O King of Numidia,
this day was your downfall.
Did you wish upon a star?
I would your wish had been granted,
for if you'd defeated Caesàr
his poison seed would ne'er have been planted!
    If Caesar had died in the field,
      the Republic would not to him yield:
democracy would not have been supplanted!

The Ides of March

Die, Caesar, die! Ignore soothsayer grim
and on the Senate floor show your bold face
that we might stab you in the back with blades
in full sight of our peers, yes, publicly!
Tho we may pay for this deed with our lives,
our lives are a small price to pay to save
the people's rule, democracy we love.
Yes, we reject the rule of tyrant kings
regardless of the title which they claim!

So be ye dictator or Emperor,
or Kaiser, or "the People's Party Chair,"
or even if they call you "President" –
all claims to powèr based on cruel brute force
reject we from the bottom of our hearts
and we'll back up these words with bloody blades,
so say we all! And pledge we all our lives,
our property, and our sacred honor.

So, motherfucker, bleed thee on the floor,
thy life is forfeit, thou aspir'st too high;
and like the giants, by lightning struck down
to fall from cloud-high slopes of Olympus,
thy fate is sealed by thy arrogant plan.
O let that be a lesson for all time!

Recent History

The Eruption of Mt. St. Helens
5-18-20

'Twas on this day in May of 1980
our lives were changed when Mt. St. Helens blew.
The deadly eruption on May 18th
blew the top off the mountain – it much changed
the local environment for grim years.

But I recall a secondary blast
that sent an ash cloud west over my house
a week later, on May 25th morn.
When I awoke, it was still dark outside,
which was unusual for this time of year;
I thought it was early, but later learned
the ash cloud had blotted out the sunlight.
And when I went downstairs it was to find
my parents storing water from the tap
because we had a reservoir uncapped.
The deadly ash so densely filled the air
we could not leave the house for quite some time
and when we did, we had to wear a mask.
The ash-fall blanketed the world around.
It thickly coated streets, houses, and cars;
there was a layer, any time we dug
into the dirt, in all my farming days.

Silver Falls State Park

With wondrous beauty, Silver Falls State Park
of a dozen majestic waterfalls
doth make impression lasting on the sense.
The moving scene of the South Falls canyon
with its mist and deep rocky precipice
is an iconic image locally:
the second-highest Oregon waterfall
(after Multnomah Falls up in the Gorge).
Many long years ago, the story goes,
the land was privately owned, not a park;
and the owner used to host paid events
that culminated in a shocking show:
they pushed old cars over the South Falls cliff
to watch them tumble as they plummeted
spinning 'round through the air to crash and wreck,
a ruin of destruction at the base.
Where now there is a jolly shallow pool
must once have been a pile of rusty hulks
a symbol of thoughtless humanity
finding entertainment in destruction
with disregard for the environment,
short-sighted pursuit of pointless pleasure:
few of us are innocent, you know it,
it only takes the right circumstance to show it.

Rosa Parks
12-1-20.ii

On December 1, thank Rosa Parks
who had the courage to tell someone, "No."
She faced arrest, jail, and prosecution
for sitting in her own seat on the bus.
Can you imagine such segregation
as part of the law, legally enforced?
Just because it's legal, don't mean it's right!
"All people are equal under the law"
is a founding first principle, and true –
that is, it *should* be true, but to our shame
we've failed to live up to our great ideals
over, and over, and over again.
And yet, we continue to fight for them
because we believe in democracy
and the possibilities of freedom.
We believe that someday, if we all fight,
our founding principles will be applied
at last to ev'ryone; no matter who
they are, or how they look, or where they're from,
or who they worship, or how much they earn;
for we are all one, despite diff'rences –
let us celebrate what makes each unique,
rather than trying to crush the others
with discrimination and oppression
that's based on race, gender, or whatever!
There is no excuse for segregation.
Let us all sit together, and be brave:
as brave as Rosa Parks was on that day.

A Society of Trolls

We're entering a social era new
thanks to advances in technology.
Our heads are full of bullshit the trolls spew:
to hurt enemies they lie cheerfully.
They'll say anything to cause painful harm,
they want to fill the world with rot and stink:
from basement-dwellers to Russian troll farms,
their purpose is to poison how we think.
Yet still, most people think "It's just a joke,"
and join in laughing at today's target
as all around the world goes up in smoke:
brotherly love we are told to forget.
Troll hatred seeps into everyone's minds
and gets worse, the more time we spend online.

The Baby Eaters

Rather than by their values positive,
far too many online communities
are brought together by their narrative
about some scary perceived enemies.
People are brought together by villains
at whom they sling their shameless blatant lies.
"The facts no longer matter," say your friends,
"the out group is so bad, we must be right!"
Their enemies are easily accused
of eating babies, or of crimes much worse.
Their *own* behavior, they claim, is excused:
"Drive out the evil *other*, so accursed!"
We must define ourselves by love, not hate,
to heal our world and make it truly great.

2020: A Retrospective

Preamble

On this year we look back with great relief,
it's possibly the worst year of our lives!
So bad that Netflix made a mocking show:
they "Death to 2020" named the film.
And based upon that retrospective view,
I now rehearse the year's events to you!

Part I: The Horror Begins

The year began with January fires
that swept across the Australian outback.
Then Donald Trump, trying to distract us
from his impeachment trial, ordered a strike
that killed an official in far Iran
and we were all worried for a few days
of imminent nucleàr World War Three!

With all this going on, 'twas no surprise
(tho quite a shame) that after evidence
was presented showing conclusively
that Donald Trump and his conspirators
had knowingly accepted Russian help
to influence the election outcome,
and tried to besmirch his future rival
by funds withholding from Ukraine (so they
would make some splashy headlines, as he liked) –
despite it all, Senate Republicans
acquitted him and let him off scot free!

Then Covid lockdown struck us all quite hard:
the schools shut down, and businesses also.
On social media we spent too much time,
and that harmed us all psychologically;
not to mention the imminent death fear;
and the run on the world's supermarkets
resulting in global shortages
of our common household commodities
like toilet paper, and pasta, and rice,
and flour, and rubbing alcohol as well –
only our grandparents have e'er lived through
such shortages of basic staple goods,
and that was back in the Great Depression!

Throughout the lengthy lockdown, we crumbled:
on one another turned through Internet.
The infighting and backbiting extreme
drove me out of my online social group
as millions of people who seethed with rage
all cast about for convenient targets.

Part II: A Nation in Flames

But trolling our peers was inadequate,
and in late May a new target was found
for all the rage we'd pent up in lockdown,
when George Floyd was murdered on video
by a callous police officer cruel
who knelt on his neck for nine minutes long.
We seemed to teeter on perilous brink
of revolution and conflict armed
as protesters defied curfews to march
demanding just accountability:
civilian oversight of the police
who've killed too many People of Color

yet consequences for their actions faced they none;
a pattern repeated o'er many years,
systemic racism made manifest.

But after months being cooped up at home,
a noisy minority headlines made:
some came with automatic weapons
in hopes of inciting a Civil War;
some started riots and destroyed windows;
and anarchist arsonists burned buildings.
It is the default for folks in Portland
to turn "anarchist" at ev'ry protest.
They, in their White Privilege, believe
that any smash and burn is justified!
Some took their White Privilege a further step:
outlets retail like Target looted they
as cover using the George Floyd protests –
the White people blamed Black people for it.
Although looters in videos were White,
no criticism of them was allowed
by Cancel Culture hardliners online
(so fuck you, Cancel Culture, you're the worst!)
Some friends have never spoken to me since
for, they maintained, White people looting stores
was an expression of Black people's rage.
Yes, so concerned were they with taking sides,
all logic and reason left they behind.

The protests lasted through the summer long;
the buildings burned, and people screamed with rage.
Some far-right little asshole with a gun
showed up one night and murdered protesters,
shot indiscriminately into crowds,
for which Republicans called him a "hero,"
so badly has society collapsed
when QAnon is louder than the truth.

Then in late summer when the West was dry,
huge forest fires roared throughout the land
displacing thousands, as from flames we fled
all seeking refuge, in fear for our homes.
It seemed ev'rything might go up in flames.

Part III: Decisive Victory?

The smoke overshadowed Supreme Court fights.
The nation mourned belovèd RBG,
and Amy Coney Barrett was installed:
supreme hypocrisy of McConnell
who will say anything to get his way.

Attempting to prevent democracy,
Trump minions sabotaged the Post Office,
removing sorting machine equipment
and rounding up blue drop boxes in trucks,
a symbol of our times if e'er there was!
But nonetheless, after nail-biting count
it became clear: Biden the vote had won!
Republicans dislike democracy;
their mobs chanted the slogan, "Stop the count!"
For they believe only *their* votes should count,
and other people's votes should be thrown out.
They have not stopped, a danger they remain:
they stormed the Oregon State Capitol
and who knows what they'll do in this next year.
But in the end, the year came to a close
with hope for a better one coming up.
Despite snafus, the vaccine will at last
release us all from Covid's nightmare grip;
and Biden will assume his White House role
despite machinations to prevent it.

We have been damaged. We have been weakened.
The fabric of society has torn.
I no longer agree with my own side,
due to their social media behavior –
while t'other side fascist ideas adopts!
It is a sucky place for us to be;
but we strive on, and there at last is hope
again that in the future we will find
ideals together us again to bind
like cooperation, friendship, and love;
accountable to one another hold,
hypocrisy avoid, and truth be told.

The Capitol Insurrection
1-6-21.ii

A right-wing insurrection tried to seize
the seat of government by force today.
A mad mob stormed the Capitol Building
in Washington, D.C. – no mere protest,
an act of insurrection violent!
The Joint Chambers were into hiding forced,
prevented from confirming vote tally:
doing the bidding of the "President"
who holds himself above the law, always.
We should not be surprised by these events.
The MAGAs have been working t'wards it now
throughout the long years since twenty-sixteen.
They do not believe in democracy;
that's why for Trump they voted, after all.
They told us all along they'd not accept
election results, unless their guy won –
we cannot be surprised they won't accept
election results, now that their guy lost.

Assassinated Caesar was the first
of a long line of Emperors of Rome:
his death did not restore democracy.
It's not a course we wish to emulate.
Our peaceful transfer is what makes us great –
we still can save it; it is not too late.

The Second Impeachment of Donald Trump
2-9-21

'Twas here in Or'gon that it all began,
the second day of Two Thousand Sixteen.
Incited by haters from out of state,
a mob with automatic rifles armed
invaded the Malheur Wildlife Refuge:
national park, a habitat for birds,
protected public lands outside of Burns.
The terrorists invaded the refuge,
at gunpoint held it for 41 days.
They fences bulldozed, offices ransacked,
they stole equipment, destroyed property,
and threatened to kill any who opposed.
If they had not been White, they'd have been shot!
When one of their leaders tried to escape
and intercepted by police he was,
he reached for his gun, intent on murder:
he would have killed a police officer
if the officer had not shot him first.
They played the victim, those armed aggressors,
despite the FBI's gentle treatment.
A jury of my peers sided with them:
acquitted terrorists, to lasting shame.
The leaders of the group were let off, free!
There was no justice, no justice at all.

Then twelve days later, Trump was ēlectèd:
he rode that sentiment of anarchy,
and tried so hard a dictator to be:
for in the absence of a government,

the rule of warlords will always take hold,
and some assholes like it better that way.
He never cared about democracy,
'twas clear from the beginning of his term.
Rejecting mass appeal and compromise,
he rallied up his hater base with hate
'gainst immigrants, and racial groups, and truth,
and women, and decency, and the law.
When four years later Trump th' election lost,
refused he to accept the results true
and spent two months spewing his baseless lies
because he did not care 'bout what was right
but only wanted power to retain.
Attempted he rebellion to incite!
For hours it seemed that he succeeded had.
The haters stormed the Congress in their rage,
intent on murdering the leaders true.
Had they succeeded in their violent goals,
there's no doubt that they surely would have killed
Pelosi, AOC, and even Pence;
and ev'ryone with whom they disagreed.
And as it was, two policemen they killed:
those haters who claim to support police
were screaming "Fuck the blue!" and "Traitor pigs!" –
assaulted they police with a flag pole.
The angry mob was chanting, "Stop the steal!"
by which they meant, "End this democracy!"
No reas'nable person really believes
the lies that Trump repeats about the vote.
A lie repeated oft is still a lie.
And Trump intended that his lies would send
his angry mob the Congress to attack.
It was intentional. He watched with glee
events unfolding on television
in hopes at last he could seize total pow'r.
At last he learned it would not be enough:

advisors who had better sense than he
convinced him, ask the mob depart from hence.
Remorse showed he none, regret not at all:
continued he instead his baseless lies,
attacks upon our grand democracy.

Today the Senate has Trump's trial commenced:
the second time that he has been impeached.
Impeachment managers showed video,
a montage of the violent mob that day.
A most disturbing sight it was to see:
that viōlent attempt to overthrow
this democratic government of ours
and to supplant it with dictatorship
for Donald Trump's authoritarian rule.
But we all know, before this even starts,
the Senate trial will Trump "not guilty" find,
because the Senators are chickenshit
and fear that Trump's mad mob will take revenge
if they should dare to stand up for what's right.
They're joined in unity by naked fear.
There is no hope for justice in this case,
no consequences Trump shall ever face
despite his open acts of treason high.
Acquitted Trump will be, to lasting shame.
There is no justice, no justice at all.

I ask you now: if we cannot convict
that traitor Donald Trump, who did incite
rebellion 'gainst these, our United States:
what business have we ever to convict
anyone of anything, ever again?
The Justice system is badly broken:
the innocent condemned; guilty let free.
The very concept of "justice" is fraud.
There is no justice, no justice at all.

Defeats & Victories

Aristides

Called "Just" by ancient Greeks, Aristides
    was praised for doing what was right
but in our public sphere modernity,
    all praise goes to revenge and spite.

When we unto our core ideals look back,
    the contrast could not be more stark.
It's clear, we spirit's greatness sadly lack
    when all we care about is snark.

By cynicism nothing is untouched,
    and everything can be torn down
by social media mobs, who don't do much
    but hate, and hate, and hate, and frown.

But then, we upon hist'ry may reflect
    that the ancients were no more wise
than we, for they votèd, and did reject
    Aristides, they ostracized!

The Battle of Lake Trasimene

O! Divine power of the Mind
　　to which our abilities we owe
memory and planning, love and hate,
　　our hopes, and thoughts we'd rather forego.
Imagination, creativity,
　　skills, talents, hopes, and fears,
our attitudes and ability,
　　laughter and joy, the pain and tears.
You're always going, you never stop,
　　and sometimes being active is good.
You're always going, you never stop,
　　and sometimes we really wish you would.
O! Goddess of Mind personified
　　the ancients sang praises to you
when Rome lived in dread of Hannibal
　　and their leaders didn't know what to do.

On this day in history, June the 8th,
　　the Roman Senators resolved
that vows unto Mind they would undertake
　　and afterwards their problems were solved.

Hard times had fallen, prospects were bleak
　　when Flaminius Consul was killed,
his army utterly defeated
　　by mighty Hannibal, strong-willed.

Of this battle, more detail we learn
　　from historian soldier more recent:
a Civil War vet'ran named T. A. Dodge,
　　who fought for the North, as was decent.

From ancient sources Dodge reconstructs
   Hannibal's battles in great detail.
That wasn't enough, so he went there himself
   the sites of those great battles to surveil.

Thus Dodge with confidence can state
   how Hannibal chose his battlefield
and fell upon Flaminius in a tight place
   when Lake Trasimene's mist concealed.

But Hannibal's strategy was cautious,
   and he chose not to march upon Rome,
much to the relief of his enemies,
   who'd feared him invading their home.

The Romans appointed a dictator
   to them through emergency lead
(the position was only temporary
   prior to Julius Caesar's greed).

Dictator Fabius Maximus decided
   battle with Hannibal to avoid;
and to this plan he stuck a long time
   even though many were annoyed:

Because Hannibal always won in the field,
   and Fabius could not hope to defeat
such a brilliant general head-on;
   instead, he decided not to compete.

It was in this way Rome eventually won,
   with time wearing Hannibal down;
and all because goddess *Mens*, the Mind,
   provided advice that was sound.

The Defeat of the Fabii
February 13

i.

But why would Ovid tell his battle tale
so out of place, as all the scholars say?
If Livy and sev'ral others all date
the battle to July, why tell it here?
If all of Rome was well aware back then
of famous histōry Ovid recites,
he could not have intended them to fool –
perhaps blowback he might have expected!
Could he have merely wanted this grand chance
to flaunt his oratory in Book Two
instead of waiting 'til July 18,
a book he ne'er did formally complete?
Or was he trying power to appease
(as so oft seems the case after disgrace)
by separating this tale from its date,
and thereby sparing an embarassment
to the patrician fam'ly then so high
whose ancestors suffered shameful defeat?
Or could the armchair historian famed have erred?
Perhaps Livy's mistaken, Ovid correct![1]

---

1   Ovid and Livy were contemporaries, and both sometimes had a propensity
    to, shall we say, tell a story the way they wanted it to sound. Of the two,
    Livy is perhaps more likely to have directly repeated what someone else
    told him, while Ovid is more likely to have carefully consider the finer
    points and implications. Julius Caesar had substantially revised the Roman
    calendar, implementing the system we now call the Julian Calendar.
    Before that, the Roman calendar was subject to politicized wranglings and
    often grossly failed to synchronize with the standard year. One might
    hypothesize that Ovid had troubled to calculate the correct date of the
    defeat of the Fabii in accordance with the new Julian Calendar, whereas
    Livy had uncritically repeated the date written in his old manuscripts.

ii.

So arrogantly the Romans marched out
to war, believing none could them defeat.
The ruling fam'ly of the Fabii
had gathered up an army of soldiers,
three hundred marched out of the city gates,
a small division by our modern terms,
intending neighbor Tuscans to attack.
The River Cremera was then in flood,
says Ovid, from the heavy winter rains.
And by its banks they pitched a camp, then charged!
Their rush pierced the Etruscan lines, men fled,
the Romans stabbed them in the back with glee.
Believing they had won the victory,
they jumped for joy to celebrate success.
Numerically superior Tuscans
did then regroup, surrounding Roman flanks.
Then Romans did regret flood at their back!
They had nowhere to go. They could not win.
Their arrogance was repaid with the sword.
Etruscans slaughtered Fabii that day,
and cut then down, yes, ev'ry single one,
allowing Roman blood so arrogant
to stain Cremera's flood a dirty red.

Catullus

"*Odi et amo,*" Catullus once wrote,
"I hate and I love," and the hate comes first,
making Poem 85 relatable.
Catullus is at his most human here,
passionate, tormented, voicing his pain,
speaking for me through his ancient verses.
"I love and I hurt," I also once wrote
an otherwise unremarkable poem
decades before I heard of Catullus,
"and it fills me up inside," it went on,
"I love and I hurt and it tears me apart,"
echoing Catullus, though I knew not.
"*Fieri sentio et excrucior,*"
Catullus concluded in his own work:
"I feel its onset, and it tortures me."
These feelings may not be universal,
but I know I share them with a poet
who died more than two thousand years ago,
and somehow feel a little less alone.

Lucretius

There once was a man named Lucretius
who sure was not being facetious
    when he said, "I shall show
    all we think that we know:
observe what Mother Nature can teach us!"

An Ironic Figure of Speech

Ironic 'tis, *De Rerum Natura*
opens with verse invoking a goddess,
great Venus, who sparks creation from love:
ironic because, as Lucretius knows,
the gods and goddesses are fallacies,
artificial constructs made by humans,
creations of the imagination,
as Lucretius will discuss in Book 5,
and indeed throughout the text of the poem.

Memmius

In his most famed and scientific poem,
Lucretius verse addressed to Memmius,
to him explaining the errors of thought
common to popular society
and embraced by Memmius personally.
This same Memmius is also mentioned
in the invective poems of Catullus
who reviles him for his poor leadership
(apparently for disinterest in bribes,
which amoral Catullus would have liked).
Surely these literary mentions are
a distinction Memmius did not enjoy.

Atoms and Void

Lucretius described the laws of physics
with remarkable accuracy.
Using reason to discredit mystics,
he imagined atoms and chemistry.

His accuracy was remarkable
when Lucretius described the Universe:
atoms and chemistry, deduced by reasoning subtle
and the teachings of Greek Epicurus.

The Universe, as Lucretius described,
was infinite in scope, though filled with void.
The teachings which Epicurus prescribed
kept Lucretius from getting paranoid.

Preaching infinite void and atoms mingling
instead of the gods more traditional
could have set a paranoid poet to tingling
if he feared a punitive judicial.

Although traditional gods he discredited,
in those days Rome was a Republic yet.
No punitive judicial prevented him from saying what he did
when Lucretius described the laws of physics. Let us not forget!

Just Like Us

We study Roman poetry and quote
their politicians, leaders of their realm;
romanticize their toga-draped culture;
recall that their language influenced our own:
yet all the while (convenient!) overlook
the cruelty of their culture at its core:
society of slave-owners and slaves,
an Empire of expansion, invasion!
The people celebrated such cruelty,
the bloody slaughter of pris'ners and slaves.
They loved to watch the gladiator "games,"
and built the famed majestic Coliseum
where crowds gathered to enjoy brutal death.
They had learned that they liked to see blood shed,
and wanted to see more, just not their own!
So slaves were captured and imported hence,
then trained to fight, and on each other set.
And sometimes captives were simply fodder
to lions fed, or tigers, or wild beasts,
so bored Roman crowds could savor the sight
as fellow humans suffered a cruel death.

Cultural History

Biblical Heroes

When I read the Bible
  the heroes I see
are the ones who weren't treated
  kindly by history:
Like Esau, the better brother,
  by his own family undermined;
or Shechem, foully murdered
  then slandered for all time;
or Eve, whose painful punishment
  surely did not suit her crime.

The Prophet Muhammad

Forty years old was Prophet Muhammad
when his first revelation came to him.
The beginning of the Quran he wrote,
and thus began a new phase of his life,
the phase which would define him for all time.
This is the event commemorated
by Ramadan's annual observance
during the ninth month of the lunar year,
from crescent moon to the next crescent moon.

Sin and Death

Blind poet Milton, in *Paradise Lost*[2]
describes how Satan first gave birth to Sin
when from his head she sprang, full-grown and armed
just as Athena from the head of Zeus
into splendid goddess status emerged.
Just as a thought is conceived and takes form
within the workings of the human mind,
so Sin was born when Satan took up arms,
rebelling against the patriarchy.
Th' incestuous details, incongruous
with asex cherubim elsewhere described,
convenient as a metaphor still is,
for with the Sin of which he had just thought
Satan became enamored, and conceived
the fatal offspring demon known as Death.
Just so, fixation with our darkest thoughts
and impulses may lead to our downfall.

---

2   Paradise Lost, Book II lines 746-767

The Morning Star

The Light-Bringer heralds the newborn day,
the planet Venus as the Morning Star
in ancient times was known by Pagan name
Lucifer, from "*lux*," bringer of light.
How came we to identify this star
as fallen archangel, who evil brings?
And could our modern mythology change
to accommodate the original
concept of the Morning Star Lucifer
who brings a light to shine, and so reveals
the darkness of oppressive religion,
as envisioned by the great William Blake
who penned *The Marriage of Heaven and Hell*?
Most people worship the wrong God, it's clear:
the God of hate who doth discriminate
against LGBTQ+ people,
always crying "sinner," passing judgment
when compassion should be religion's point.

The Conversion of St. Paul

One of the greatest Christian saints
    was once a sinner, too!
He made mistakes not small, but great,
    yes, just like me and you.

In the employ of conquerors
    to heretics prosecute,
he did what he had always done –
    'twas no forbidden fruit.

Saul rode the road one winter day
    when revelation struck –
described he "like a lightning bolt"
    it came as such a shock.

Then to the ground he senseless fell
    as though he'd been struck blind,
while thoughts of all the wrongs he'd done
    waged war within his mind.

The Bible contradicts itself
    whether his companions heard.
We understand it's metaphor
    when "heaven" spoke those words.

But sure it is, his life he changed,
    he turned it all around:
his job, his game, even his name
    from that event profound.

As Paul, he framed his message new
    and preached it to the masses,
'bout how his life had turned around
    while riding t'wards Damascus.

Too bad the Christians did not learn
    from old Saint Paul's mistakes:
they Jews and Mithraists did burn;
    and "witches," at the stake.

Good Friday

Only a few days after your entrance,
triumphant ride through Jerusalem's streets,
you were arrested for rabble rousing:
tried, convicted, and marched up that grim hill
accompanied by the jeers of the crowd,
the same who'd welcomed you just days before.
The iron cruel they drove through hands and feet
as painfully they nailed you to the cross,
then set it upright and left you to die.
You for your mother cried, just like George Floyd.
Then with your dying breath you said a prayer
that to your tormentors forgiveness granted,
a wish for peace such as few would have thought
while in the midst of painful anguished death.

But did your death solve anything at all?
Did those who murdered you feel better then?
By acting on their cruel judgmental hate
did those self-righteous bastards closure find?
I think we all know well that they did not.
Those such as they just move on to the next
with no remorse, just permanent outrage –
they always are convinced that they are right,
and always seek out someone else to judge.

Your followers were forced to meaning find
when thus their hopes came to untimely end,
but your forgiveness showed them all the way
'til your forgiveness was granted to all.

Now highway billboards righteously proclaim
you *chose* to die, to forgive all our sins –
if true, a form of human sacrifice!
Although your message has been mangled now,
your painful death ensured your words lived on.
It's not a choice that anyone would make.
On balance, I hope it helped more than hurt.

The Sinagua Calendar

Upon the day when sun shone through the crack,
its beam illuminated symbols carved
into the stone by ancestors so wise:
that was the day the people knew the time
had come to plant their crops in time for Spring!

The Sinagua people long ago
observed the Vernal Equinox each year
with petroglyphs they carved upon the stone
in Sacred Mountain Basin, Arizona
well over a millennia ago.
The Water Clan's Sunwatcher monitored
the movement of the sunbeam o'er the face
of a vast sandstone bluff near Beaver Creek.
More than a thousand petroglyphs were carved
into the diff'rent faces of the rock,
and many tracked positions of the Sun.
They likely used a lunar calendar
with nameless months, just as in Rome of old.

The people practiced agriculture there,
and irrigated fields with dug canals
to grow their crops of cotton, corn, and beans,
as well as squash plants with broad spreading leaves.
They built cliff dwellings, some five stories tall,
a feat of architecture far advanced!
(Although that may have been later on.)
They built a court for sports played with a ball.
The ancients weren't so different from us.

The markings on the stone quite clearly show
alignment on the Vernal Equinox
when sunbeam shafts of light made a straight line
connecting symbols on the great rock face
to show the people Springtime had begun!

finis

Errata

Any factual errors that may be found to be contained within these pages are undoubtedly my own fault, and should not be blamed on my sources.

I have made an effort to be factually accurate in all things. However, with regards to my historical poems, I may have made assumptions or faulty readings. I am foremost a poet, not a historian. I encourage the reader to find inspiration to learn about the history of our society.

In Oscar Wilde's poem, "The Ballad of Reading Gaol," the prisoners were kept in their cells during the execution of the murderer. They were not lined up in the yard to witness the hanging, as I erroneously described in my own poem. Furthermore, Oscar Wilde's poem does not mention the executioner looking the condemned man in the eye. I don't know where I got that idea. But it rhymes, dammit; so having written it, I kept the lines as they are. I hope the reader will forgive this exercise of "poetic license."

Regarding Bede: throughout the year's writing and previously, I had always assumed it was a two-syllable name with a long final vowel, as in such familiar names as Persephone, Hecate, Jesse, or anemone. It was only when watching an old episode of Doctor Who that I heard the name "Bede" spoken aloud and realized my error: everyone else pronounces his name as a single syllable, "Beed." Whoops! Rather than rewrite the poems in the dozens of places where I had used the monk's name, I used an accent symbol over the final vowel to indicate my unconventional pronunciation. I hope the serious scholars will forgive me, if they ever read any of this.

References and Resources

I referenced a number of Wikipedia entries: including articles relating to many holidays; the structure of the modern calendar; the month names of various ancient cultures; Greco-Roman gods and goddesses; historical events; and biographies of historical persons, including Casey Jones and the extended family of Augustus Caesar, among others. I have not cited all of these articles individually, but I thank Wikipedia as an invaluable resource to the layperson who wishes to pursue a variety of interests.

For current events, my primary news source is the CNN mobile app, although I have also referenced The Guardian, NPR, The Oregonian, The Statesman-Journal, The Daily Show, and a variety of less reputable sources via social media.

I gratefully referenced the following resources:

Abrams, M.H., et al., editors. (1993 ed.) *The Norton Anthology of English Literature: Sixth Edition, Volume 1.* New York, NY: W. W. Norton & Company

Bede. (trans, ed, intro, notes & commentary by Faith Wallis). (2012 ed). *Bede: The Reckoning of Time, Translated with introduction, notes and commentary by Faith Wallis.* Translated Texts for Historians, Volume 29. Liverpool, UK: Liverpool University Press. [I have tremendous respect for Professor Wallis, she has done amazing work with very thorough scholarship.]

Blake, William. (2005 ed.). *William Blake: Selected Poems.* Read by Frederick Davidson. Audiobook. Blackstone Audio, Inc. and Buck 50 Productions, LLC via Libby.

Catullus. (trans. Guy Lee). (1998 ed.) *The Poems of Catullus: Edited and translated with an Introduction and Notes by Guy Lee.* Oxford, UK: Oxford University Press (Oxford World's Classics).

Cohen, Marshall. (July 9, 2020). *'Broken heart syndrome' has increased during the Covid-19 pandemic, small study suggests.* CNN. https://www.cnn.com/2020/07/09/health/broken-heart-syndrome-coronavirus-wellness/index.html

Dickinson, Emily. (Christanne Miller, ed.). (2016). *Emily Dickinson's Poems As She Preserved Them.* Cambridge, MA: The Belknap Press of Harvard University Press.

Dodge, Theodore Ayrault. (orig. 1889, 2005 ed.) *Hannibal: Introduction by Ian M. Cuthbertson.* New York, NY: Barnes & Noble, Inc.

Epicurus (George K. Strodach, trans. & introd., foreword by Daniel Klein). (2012 ed.) *The Art of Happiness.* New York, NY: Penguin Books (Penguin Group USA, Inc.)

Frost, Robert. (1969 ed.) *The Poetry of Robert Frost: Edited by Edward Connery Lathem.* New York: Holt, Rinehart and Winston.

Lucretius. (Ronald Melville, trans.). (2008 ed.). *On the Nature of the Universe: A verse translation by Ronald Melville, with an Introduction and Notes by Don and Peta Fowler.* Oxford, UK: Oxford University Press (Oxford World's Classics).

Maudslay, Francesca (director). (2010). *When Rome Ruled: War Machine.* National Geographic Television, DVD. Universal City, CA: Vivendi Entertainment (Distributor).

Milton, John. (John Leonard, ed. & introd.). (2003 ed.) *Paradise Lost.* New York, NY: Penguin Books.

Ovid. (trans, ed, intro & notes Peter Green). (2005 ed.). *The Poems of Exile: Tristia and the Black Sea Letters, With a New Foreword; Translated with an Introduction, Notes, and Glossary by Peter Green.* Berkeley, CA: University of California Press.

Ovid. (Anne & Peter Wiseman, trans, ed, & notes). (2013 ed.). *Fasti.* Oxford, UK: Oxford University Press (Oxford World's Classics).

Ovid. (trans. A.D. Melville, intro & notes E.J. Kenney; translation of "The Art of Love" by B. P. Moore with revisions by A.D. Melville). (2008 ed.) *The Love Poems.* Oxford, UK: Oxford University Press (Oxford World's Classics). [This rhyming verse translation includes all of Ovid's famous transgressive works of "love" poetry, for which he was later exiled: *Amores, Cosmetics for Ladies, Ars Amatoria,* and *Remedia Amatoria.*]

Smith, Jesse S. (2008 ed.). *Principles for a Self-Directed Society.* Portland, OR: Basementia Publications.

Smith, Jesse S. (2016 ed.). *Rise of the Pagans.* Silverton, Oregon: Basementia Publications.

Shakespeare, William. (2005 ed.) *The Sonnets: Read by Alex Jennings.* Audiobook. Naxos AudioBooks via Libby.

Tyson, Neil de Grasse. (2017). *Astrophysics for People in a Hurry: Read by the Author / Unabridged.* Audiobook. Blackstone Publishing via Libby.

Various/unknown. (trans. Division of Christian Education of the National Council of the Churches of Christ in the United States of America). (1959 ed.). *The Holy Bible: Revised Standard Version containing the Old and New Testaments, Translated from the Original Tongues.* Camden, NJ: Thomas Nelson Inc.

Zoll, Kenneth J. (2008). *Sinagua Sunwatchers: An Archaeoastronomy Survey of the Sacred Mountain Basin.* Sedona, AZ: Sunwatcher Publishing.